The Library of PIRATES™

Captain Kidd

Seventeenth-Century Pirate of the Indian Ocean and African Coast

Aileen Weintraub

The Rosen Publishing Group's
PowerKids Press™
New York

To my DaddyMonster, who was the most fearless of them all

Published in 2002 by The Rosen Publishing Group, Inc.
29 East 21st Street, New York, NY 10010

First Edition

Book Design: Michael Caroleo and Michael de Guzman
Project Editors: Jennifer Landau, Jason Moring, Jennifer Quasha
Consultant: Ken Kinkor

Photo Credits: p. 4 © SuperStock; pp. 7, 8, 11, 16 (Captain Kidd) © Mary Evans Picture Library; p.12 © Bettmann/CORBIS; pp. 15 (background pirates), 19 © North Wind Pictures; p. 15 (silk) © Kevin R. Morris/CORBIS; p. 15 (gun) © National Maritime Museum Picture Library; p. 16 (treasure chest) © Index Stock; p. 20 (Parliament) © E.O. Hoppe/CORBIS; p. 20 (Captain Kidd) © CORBIS.

Weintraub, Aileen, 1973–
    Captain Kidd : seventeenth-century pirate of the Indian ocean and African coast/ Aileen Weintraub.
        p. cm. — (The library of pirates)
    Includes bibliographical references
    ISBN 0–8239–5797–7 (lib. bdg.)
    1. Kidd, William. d. 1701—Juvenile literature. 2. Pirates-Biography—Juvenile literature. [1. Kidd, William. d. 1701. 2. Pirates.] I. Title.
    G537.K5 W39 2002
    910.4'5–dc21

00–013012

Manufactured in the United States of America

Contents

This painting shows William Kidd (far right) in New York Harbor. Kidd never thought of himself as a pirate.

Life Before Piracy

William Kidd was **infamous** for his pirating activities on the Indian Ocean, off the coast of Africa, during the late 1600s. Kidd was born in Scotland around 1645. Not much is known about his early life except that his father was a **Presbyterian** minister. By 1689, Kidd had become a **privateer** for the British. A privateer is paid by the government to **plunder** enemy ships. Kidd fought against French warships off the island of Saint Martin. In 1691, he went to New York and married a woman named Sarah Oort. Together they had two daughters. For a while, Kidd earned a living as an honest businessman. In time he became bored with this kind of life. In 1695, he left his family and sailed to England looking for adventure.

Captain Kidd Makes a Deal

While in London, Kidd met two men, Robert Livingstone and Lord Bellamont. Both of these men were government officials. The three came up with a plan. They would buy a ship, sail to the Indian Ocean, and capture pirates who were selling stolen goods. Bellamont and Livingstone would give Kidd money for the voyage, and Kidd would command the ship. Kidd got a **letter of marque** from the government saying he could attack any ships that were at war with England. William III, the king of England, signed a **warrant** to let Kidd keep anything he captured from enemy ships. This was strange because privateers usually gave part of the prizes to the government. The king agreed to this only because he secretly was offered a share of whatever was captured.

This picture shows men seated around a model of a sailing ship. The ship shown is from 1750, about 100 years past Kidd's time.

The *Adventure Galley*

The ship chosen for Kidd's voyage to the Indian Ocean was the *Adventure Galley*. The ship weighed 287 tons (260 t), and measured 125 feet (38.1 m) long. It was armed with 34 guns. The anchor alone weighed 1 ½ tons (1.4 t). Kidd sailed from England to New York with 80 men. While in New York, he found more men looking for adventure. On September 6, 1696, Captain Kidd began his journey with 152 men. On January 27, 1697, they landed in Tulear, a small port on the coast of Madagascar. The crew stayed there for a month. This gave them time to rest after their long journey. Soon they restocked the ship with fresh food and water and set sail once again.

◀ *This is a picture of Captain Kidd aboard the Adventure Galley. Howard Pyle, the artist, was famous for his drawings of pirates.*

No Purchase, No Pay

Captain Kidd had an agreement with his crew. This was called the No Purchase, No Pay agreement. This meant that the only way crew members would get paid was if they captured other ships. If the crew didn't find ships to plunder, they would go home without any riches. This was a big risk to take. As the voyage continued, the crew could not find any ships to plunder. Kidd was getting **desperate**. He decided to capture any ships he could find. This was not part of the agreement he had with the British government. Kidd knew he could get in trouble. In August 1697, Kidd tried to take over a ship on the Red Sea. The captain spotted the *Adventure Galley*, fired guns, and yelled threats at Kidd's crew. Kidd lost his courage and backed off.

This picture shows pirates fighting off an enemy. In the same way, a ship on the Red Sea fought off the men of the Adventure Galley.

Out of Luck

Captain Kidd's crew was getting angry. They wanted to see some rewards for their efforts. The *Adventure Galley* began to leak and supplies were running low. About 30 men died of **tropical** diseases. Many of the crew had scurvy. This is a disease caused by a lack of vitamin C. Kidd was finding it hard to control his crew. They didn't respect him and more than once they almost decided to **mutiny**. On October 30, 1697, Kidd and a crew member named William Moore had a fight. Kidd ended up killing Moore by hitting him over the head with an iron bucket. The situation on the *Adventure Galley* was hard to endure. Something had to be done.

◀ *This picture shows Captain Kidd hitting William Moore over the head with a bucket. Kidd thought he had a right to kill Moore because Moore had not listened to Kidd.*

13

A Fantastic Fortune

The *Adventure Galley* came across a small trading ship off the Malabar Coast of India. Kidd fired a shot. He took over the small ship and stole the **booty**. This still wasn't enough to satisfy his men. On January 30, 1698, Kidd came across a large merchant ship called the *Quedagh Merchant*. This ship was filled with fine silk, **calico**, sugar, and precious metals. Ships often carried flags of many different countries to avoid getting attacked. To trick the ship, Kidd flew a French flag. The crew of the *Quedagh Merchant*, which was owned by the English, flew the French flag in return. They did this hoping Kidd would treat them as a friend, not an enemy. However, Kidd had permission to attack French ships. Even though Kidd knew this ship wasn't really French, he attacked. Kidd finally had found his fortune.

The large picture shows pirates taking over a ship. On the top right is a picture of colored silk. The bottom right shows a gun called a flintlock.

Declared a Pirate

Captain Kidd now had money and started attacking any ship he could find. News spread that Kidd was illegally attacking ships. It turned out that the *Quedagh Merchant* was sailing for the Dutch East India Company. This company was angry about what had happened to its ship and wanted to get back at Kidd. By April 1699, Kidd had abandoned the *Adventure Galley* for the *Quedagh Merchant*. He renamed the ship the *Adventure Prize*. He sailed to the island of Anguilla in the West Indies with a crew of 20 men. This was all that remained of his original crew. It was in Anguilla that Kidd learned that the English government had **declared** him a pirate.

◄ *On the far left is a picture of pirate's booty, including bars of gold, called bullion. The large picture shows Captain Kidd guarding his treasure as his crew prepares to bury it.*

Captured and Betrayed

Kidd sailed to the Danish island of Saint Thomas in the Caribbean. He needed a place to hide out. The governor of the island refused to protect him. Kidd then sailed to Hispaniola, now called the Dominican Republic. In Hispaniola, he bought a boat, called the *Saint Antonio*. He decided to sail to New York to see his family because he had been three years at sea. Kidd tried to make a deal with Lord Bellamont, who originally had been his partner. Bellamont promised to get Kidd a **pardon**. This was a trick. Instead Bellamont arrested Kidd for piracy. He planned to take part of Kidd's treasure. Kidd was sent back to England. He **insisted** he was innocent.

When Captain Kidd was arrested, he said that his crew made him commit piracy.

Kidd's Fate Is Sealed

Kidd was thrown in prison in England. He was locked up by himself and was not allowed to have a lawyer. On March 27, 1701, he was ordered to explain his actions to the English **Parliament**. He is the only pirate in history who had to do that. His trial was set for May. He asked for certain papers and French passes to prove that he had permission to plunder French ships. Kidd never got the passes and papers. They seemed to have disappeared mysteriously. Kidd was faced with a list of charges. Without any **evidence**, he could not prove his case. He was going to hang.

◄ *This picture shows Captain Kidd hanging in Execution Dock in London. After he died, Kidd was left hanging to remind other pirates what would happen to them if they continued to break the law.*

The Legendary Treasure

William Kidd was hanged at Execution Dock in Wapping, London, on May 23, 1701. He did not die easily. The rope snapped twice. When he finally died, the people of the town **tarred and feathered** his body. They left him hanging in an iron cage. His body stayed this way for years as a warning to others. After Kidd died, the hunt began for his treasure. The government thought it was in areas of Boston, New York, and the West Indies. Part of his treasure was found, but even today most of it remains hidden. Some think his fortune is buried on Gardiners Island on Long Island, New York. **Legend** has it that the treasure can be dug up only by three people at midnight when the moon is full. Many have tried, but no one has ever found Kidd's treasure.

Glossary

booty (BOO-tee) Prizes stolen by force.

calico (KA-lih-koh) A cotton fabric printed with small designs.

declared (dee-KLEHRD) Announced officially.

desperate (DES-puh-rit) Feeling as if one has no hope.

evidence (EH-vih-dints) Proof that something is true.

infamous. (IN-fuh-mus) Famous for doing a bad thing.

insisted (in-SIST-ed) To have said something in a forceful way.

legend (LEH-jend) A story passed down through the years that many people believe.

letter of marque (LEH-ter UV MARK) Written authority given to a person by a government to steal goods from other countries.

mutiny (MYOO-tin-ee) When a crew of a ship refuses to obey the captain.

pardon (PAR-din) The excusing of an offense.

Parliament (PAR-lih-ment) The group of people in England who make laws for their country.

plunder (PLUN-der) To rob by force.

Presbyterian (prez-buh-TEER-ee-an) A type of religion whose members believe in Jesus Christ and the Bible.

privateer (pry-vuh-TEER) An armed pirate licensed by the government to attack enemy ships.

tarred and feathered (TARD AND FEH-therd) To have smeared someone with tar and covered him with feathers, as punishment.

tropical (TRAH-puh-kul) Having to do with the warm parts of Earth that are near the equator.

warrant (WOR-ent) A piece of paper giving someone the authority to do something.

Index

Web Sites

To learn more about Captain Kidd check out these Web sites:

http://library.thinkquest.org/16438/fact/pirates/captain.htm

www.bio.umass.edu/biology/conn.river/kidd.html